I0479449

Table of Contents

MKM Creations, a culinary treasure in New Orleans.

MKM Creations stands out as a culinary gem in the center of New Orleans, providing a dining experience that is both flavorful and rooted in the city's diverse cultural past. This remarkable restaurant, noted for its broad and tasty menu, allows guests to enjoy a feast of beautifully prepared meals. From the time guests walk in, they are surrounded by the tempting fragrances of BBQ chicken, shrimp spaghetti, and other delectable delicacies, setting the stage for a wonderful lunch that embraces the spirit of New Orleans food.

The food of MKM Creations showcases culinary artistry and innovation. Signature dishes like the luscious BBQ chicken, which has the ideal smokey flavor, and the creamy, spicy shrimp pasta demonstrate the restaurant's dedication to employing high-quality ingredients and traditional techniques. For those looking for a one-of-a-kind and luxury experience, the 24k gold French toast is a delicious take on a classic favorite, combining rich, buttery flavors with a hint of extravagance. Seafood lovers will enjoy the fresh, precisely cooked lobster and crab legs, while meat eaters will appreciate the substantial, beautifully grilled T-bone steaks.

Aside from its famed in-house dining, MKM Creations specializes in catering services for a wide range of occasions, from intimate gatherings to huge festivities.

Whether it's a wedding, corporate event, or holiday party, the catering team guarantees that every dish is perfectly cooked and beautifully presented, with the same degree of expertise and attention to detail as the restaurant.

MKM Creations has swiftly established a superb reputation for both its outstanding food and its unwavering commitment to client satisfaction, distinguishing it in New Orleans' vibrant culinary scene.

Atlanta's Very Own

JOSE GUAPO

Jose Guapo, Atlanta's own rap legend, continues to make waves in the music industry with his highly anticipated new mixtape, "SFTA". Jose Guapo, known for his distinct flow and irresistible charisma, has long been a significant presence in the rap scene, continuously creating music that appeal to both fans and critics. His upcoming project, "SFTA," promises to be another masterpiece, displaying his growth as an artist while remaining faithful to the gritty, real sound that has gained him a passionate audience.

Jose Guapo's remarkable record demonstrates his consistent brilliance and innovation. My personal favorites are "ETS pt 1" and the "LJ" series (parts 1, 2, and 3 LLM), which highlight his poetic talent and ability to create interesting scenarios. Jose Guapo's "SFTA" fascinates his audience once more, merging creative beats with cutting, intelligent lyrics. Jose Guapo's reputation as a significant participant in the Atlanta rap industry and beyond grows as he continues to push boundaries and deliver outstanding songs.

Divine Bloodline
Demon Queen δ Δ

BeastSupreme
TheDuke

Destroy

くお願いします！
Will

BEST MMORPG OF ALL TIME

PHANTASY STAR UNIVERSE CLEMENTINE: THE PINNACLE OF MMORPG EXPERIENCES

Dive into the best MMORPG experience with Phantasy Star Universe Clementine, a private server that has elevated the popular PSU: Ambition of the Illuminus to new heights. This server is more than just a nostalgia trip for PSU veterans; it's a complete remake that improves every facet of the original game. From the gorgeous graphics to the enhanced gameplay mechanics, Clementine creates an immersive universe in which every decision you make might shape your future. Whether you're revisiting old experiences or exploring this realm for the first time, Clementine promises a dynamic and entertaining role-playing experience unlike any other.

Character customisation is enhanced in PSU Clementine. Become the most acclaimed healer, an indestructible tank, a merciless killer, or explore the unique hybrid classes that combine numerous roles for unrivaled flexibility. The ability to enhance your character's skills in numerous ways allows you to personalize your playstyle to exactly meet your strategic preferences. This amount of personalization is unparalleled, allowing you to design a genuinely unique hero within the enormous Phantasy Star universe.

For those looking for the ultimate challenge, Clementine has included a Hardcore Mode that tests the limits of typical MMORPG gaming. In this mode, all experience boosts are always active, hastening your progress and making each triumph sweeter. However, the stakes are high: if your character dies without a spare life, they will be lost forever. This risk-reward dynamic adds an exciting twist to your trip, making every decision vital and every encounter a test of your abilities and tactics. Are you brave enough to confront this ruthless mode and etch your name into the stone of Clementine's legends?

Join the legions of guardians who have already found the unrivalled thrills of Phantasy Star Universe Clementine. Download the game now, and invite your friends to join you on this epic voyage. Explore enormous landscapes, fight in intense battles, and form lasting partnerships. Every moment in Clementine is an opportunity to prove that you are the ultimate hero. The Gurhal is waiting for you; your adventure begins right now.

SOIL TO STUDIO: BROOKLYN'S BRIDGE TO ARTISANAL ELEGANCE.

Soil to workshop, located in the bustling borough of Brooklyn, is a textile design workshop that combines contemporary aesthetics with traditional workmanship. Based on a vision of sustainable and ethical production, this studio works together with experienced craftsmen in India to make stunning table linens, sumptuous fabrics, handcrafted bedding, and simple yet elegant everyday items. Each sculpture represents the careful creativity and cultural legacy that Soil to Studio proudly promotes.

Soil to Studio's philosophy is based on its close links with Indian craftspeople. By nurturing these collaborations, the studio guarantees that each product communicates a story about legacy and talent. The table linens and fabrics have elaborate patterns and designs that reflect India's rich textile heritage. Handcrafted bedding sets ooze comfort and elegance, with a distinctive blend of modern design and traditional processes. This dedication to authenticity and quality is visible in every creation, making Soil to Studio a shining example of handmade perfection.

SOIL TO STUDIO

Swati, the creator behind Soil to Studio, sees the studio as more than a business; it is a journey. Her commitment to sustainable techniques and ethical relationships fuels the studio's activities. "Soil to Studio is and will remain a journey," she explains, highlighting the studio's spirit of constant discovery and growth. This journey is about more than just making beautiful items; it's also about cultivating a deeper appreciation for the artists' talent and passion. It's a trip that connects Indian soil to Brooklyn's studios and homes, linking cultures and crafts.

Soil to Studio's effect extends beyond its stunning products. It is about building a community of craftspeople and ensuring that their traditions flourish in a modern marketplace. By introducing these handcrafted objects to a worldwide audience, Soil to Studio promotes sustainable livelihoods and the cultural importance of Indian workmanship. For individuals looking for one-of-a-kind, ethically manufactured textiles that combine artistry with everyday usefulness, Soil to Studio has a line that exudes elegance, integrity, and a feeling of community as we work to make the world more sustainable and beautiful.

"EXPERIENCE THE RAW POWER OF HOLLI D BARZZ FROM CHICAGO'S LOWEND WITH HER NEW SINGLE 'WAR' A PREVIEW OF THE UPCOMING TAPE 'WASTED BARZZ.'"

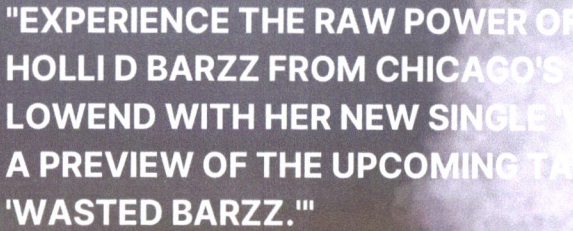

Meet Holli D Barzz, a strong rap artist from Chicago's low-income neighborhoods whose raw and real storytelling captivates audiences all over. Holli D Barzz, known for her insightful lyrics and forceful delivery, has carved herself a distinct place in the rap world with her outspoken style and engaging stories. Her latest single, "War," exemplifies her ability to combine harsh realism with striking beats, providing listeners with a profound view into her life's difficulties and accomplishments, as well as the world around her.

"War" is the lead single from her new project, "Wasted Barzz," which aims to push boundaries and challenge norms. The record is a hard-hitting anthem that embodies the spirit of Holli D Barzz's struggles and the never-ending struggle for survival and prosperity. With its strong beats and thought-provoking lyrics, "War" foreshadows what fans may anticipate from "Wasted Barzz"—a raw, unedited voyage through the highs and lows of life in Chicago's lowlands.

Holli
D
Barzz

Holli D Barzz's music distinguishes out for both its lyrical depth and emotional impact. Her ability to express personal pain and societal challenges via compelling music has gained her a devoted audience. Each song on "Wasted Barzz" is expected to delve deeply into themes of suffering, tenacity, and perseverance, reflecting both her personal experiences and the larger context of her community. Her storytelling is more than just painting a picture; it is also about eliciting a visceral response, having her audience feel every word and beat.

As fans wait for the release of "Wasted Barzz," Holli D Barzz continues to create waves in the business. Her unique voice and rigorous approach to rap are distinguishing her in a crowded field. With "War" already making an effect, it's evident that Holli D Barzz is on the path to stardom. Her new album promises to be a watershed moment, cementing her reputation as a rising artist and a forceful voice from Chicago's lowend. Keep an eye on Holli D Barzz as she prepares to release "Wasted Barzz" and further her rise in the rap industry.

WHO IS JT HUSSLE OF TIMELESS BEAUTY BOUTIQUE?

TIMELESS BEAUTY BOUTIQUE: JT HUSSLE'S FASHION HAVEN IN CHICAGO.

In Chicago's booming fashion scene, Timeless Beauty Boutique, run by the fashionable and ambitious JT Hussle, has carved out a unique niche. This online shop features a carefully curated range of stylish apparel that represents both modern style and timeless elegance. JT Hussle's acute sense of fashion and commitment to quality have made Timeless Beauty Boutique a must-visit destination for fashion-forward individuals looking to upgrade their wardrobe.

Timeless Beauty Boutique has an outstanding clothing selection that caters to a wide range of tastes and preferences. From sleek and classy jumpsuits to adaptable denim sets, the boutique has items that can easily transition from day to night. Her cargo pants range mixes functionality with modern flair, resulting in an ideal balance of comfort and style. As the seasons change, Timeless Beauty Boutique keeps clients ahead of the trend curve with their comfortable and beautiful puff jackets, which are ideal for fighting the cold Chicago weather in style.

JT Hussle's mission for Timeless Beauty Boutique goes beyond merely selling trendy items; she wants to create an unforgettable shopping experience. The boutique's warm atmosphere, along with customized customer attention, makes every visit unique. JT's love of fashion and dedication to her customers are visible in every part of the store, from the meticulously curated inventory to the attentive style advise provided to customers. Her hands-on approach guarantees that each customer discovers things that not only look fantastic, but also make them feel confident and powerful.

The success of Timeless Beauty Boutique is a credit to JT Hussle's entrepreneurial energy and extensive knowledge of the fashion business. Her business has become a renowned feature in Chicago's retail environment, earning a devoted following and receiving glowing reviews. Whether you're looking for the right dress for a special occasion or simply want to update your wardrobe, Timeless Beauty Boutique has a varied assortment of high-quality, stylish clothing to meet all of your fashion needs. Discover why Timeless Beauty Boutique is a must-see site for Chicago's fashion fans.

1100 HIMSELF

DIVE INTO THE POWERFUL SOUNDS AND RAW SKILL OF OAKLAND'S OWN 1100 HIMSELF, A RISING RAP SENSATION WHO IS TAKING THE MUSIC LANDSCAPE BY STORM.

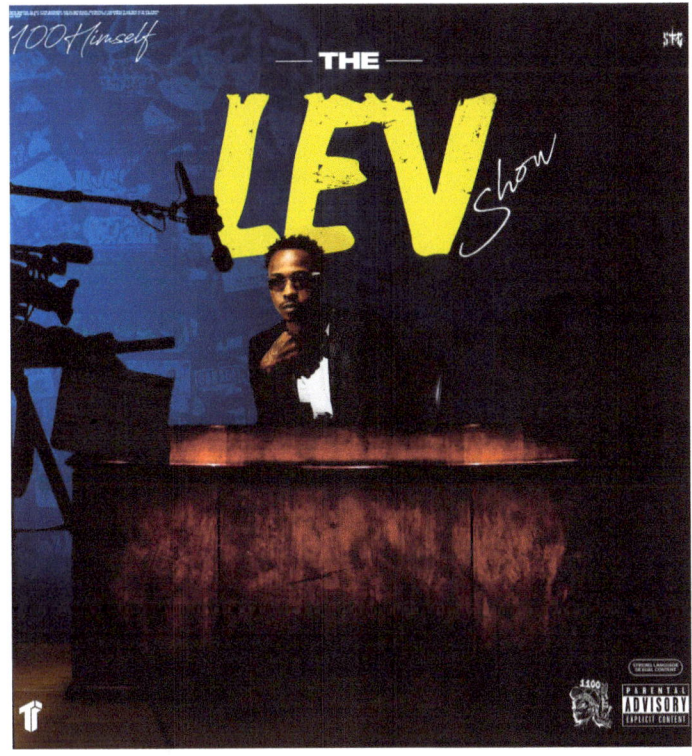

From the streets of Oakland, California, rises a budding hip-hop star: 1100 Himself. 1100 Himself is creating a name for himself in the music industry with his unique blend of dope beats and compelling samples, which can be heard on his cassettes "Funk Theft Auto" and "2 Headed Goat," both beautifully produced by the great Mitchell. His tracks captivate listeners with appealing rhythms and thought-provoking lyrics that represent his experiences and goals.

However, 1100 Himself is more than simply a one-dimensional artist; he is a multidimensional talent who enjoys diversity. Aside from his hard-hitting compositions, he's known for his sweet, melodic songs tailored just for the women, exhibiting a depth and range that distinguishes him from his colleagues. Furthermore, his love of anime lends an intriguing dimension to his demeanor, engaging with followers who share his enthusiasm for the art form. Now, with his latest project, "The Lev Show," 1100 Himself is pushing boundaries and redefining what it means to be an artist in the ever-changing world of hip hop.

1100's journey is one of personal development, creativity, and unwavering commitment to his profession. As he navigates the complexity of the music industry, he remains committed to his goal of greatness, using his platform to inspire and elevate people along the way. With his unflinching dedication to sincerity and incredible talent, 1100 Himself is ready to make an unforgettable mark on the hip-hop landscape, demonstrating that genuine artistry transcends no limits.

Meet 2Deep. The Southern President: Memphis' Multitalented Maestro

making colors work for you

Few artists embrace Memphis' rich artistic tradition more dynamically than 2 Deep The Southern President. 2 Deep, known for his electric stage presence and lyrical prowess, has become a household name in the Southern rap genre. His music exudes sincerity and a strong connection to his past, capturing the soul of Memphis' rich musical heritage. However, his abilities transcend far beyond the microphone, demonstrating a versatility that distinguishes him from his colleagues.

Aside from his impressive musical career, 2 Deep is also a skilled professional painter. His visual art, like his music, is a vivid reflection of his experiences and feelings. Each brushstroke tells a tale, with the same raw honesty and passion as his words. His paintings, which are frequently inspired by the colorful energy and soul of Memphis, have received critical acclaim and a devoted following among art fans. This combined skill has established him as a standout figure in the artistic community, flawlessly integrating the realms of music and visual art.

The recent release of his single, "Cold on the Microphone," is just another milestone in 2 Deep's long career. The tune reflects his artistic development, combining incisive lyrical content with inventive production. "Cold on the Microphone" demonstrates not just his technical prowess but also his ability to express profound, resonating messages through his music. The single has received rave reviews, cementing his position as one of Memphis' most captivating musical voices.

His story exemplifies the strength of adaptability and dedication. Whether he's writing sophisticated rhymes or making stunning visual art, his dedication to his profession is unshakeable. As he keeps pushing boundaries and exploring new artistic paths, 2 Deep The Southern President remains a key character in Memphis' artistic landscape. His work, both musical and visual, celebrates the city's unique cultural fabric, and he serves as a source of inspiration for young artists worldwide.

All Crowns Beauty Supply

All Crowns Beauty Supply in Raleigh, owned by a Christian couple from Chicago and recently featured in the Triangle Tribune, offers beauty with heart.

Fedoras
Bucket hats

SHOP NOW

Allcrowns
Beauty

Step into All Crowns Beauty Supply, a thriving beauty sanctuary in the center of Raleigh, North Carolina. All Crowns Beauty Supply was founded by a devout Christian married couple from Chicago and has quickly become a popular destination for local beauty enthusiasts. This store has a warm and welcoming ambiance and offers a wide choice of products, including excellent hair care products, beautiful wigs, trendy sunglasses, chic hats, smart bags, luscious lashes, and much more. Each visit promises more than simply a shopping experience; it also provides an opportunity to become a member of a community that values beauty, faith, and great service.

The Triangle Tribune recently released an uplifting interview with Latoya and her son, highlighting their dedication to their business and community. The piece described their journey from Chicago to Raleigh, emphasizing their commitment to offering high-quality beauty products while upholding strong Christian principles. Their narrative speaks to many people, demonstrating how their faith and family-oriented attitude have contributed to their success and the loyal client base they've developed.

All Crowns Beauty Supply stands out not only for its wide product offerings, but also for its individualized customer care. Latoya and her staff are dedicated about assisting each customer in finding just what they need to feel confident and beautiful. Whether you're looking for the right wig, the newest hair care innovation, or accessories to accent your appearance, All Crowns Beauty Supply is your one-stop shop. Their dedication to excellence and community distinguishes them as a bright gem in Raleigh's beauty scene, and their narrative continues to inspire and motivate everyone who passes through their doors.

DISCOVER CHIC WOMEN'S FASHION AT LEIGHAS LANE IN BRONZEVILLE, FEATURING VERSATILE TWO-PIECE SETS, JUMPSUITS, AND MORE—

Leighas Lane, located in Chicago's lively Bronzeville district, is a prominent boutique that specializes in women's fashion. Leighas Lane caters to the modern lady, offering a wide range of stylish attire, including practical one-size-fits-all two-piece sets, chic jumpsuits, warm tracksuits, and stunning dresses. Each piece is carefully chosen to exemplify both comfort and sophistication, making it simple for each lady to discover something that suits her individual style.

Customer satisfaction is first priority at Leighas Lane, as evidenced by the positive feedback on her products. Customers routinely compliment the boutique on its high-quality merchandise and excellent customer service. Whether you're looking for a casual outfit or a statement piece for a special occasion, Leighas Lane guarantees a fun shopping trip. Make sure to check out her Facebook page to see her stunning inventory and read personal tales of the boutique's exceptional goods.

LEIGHAS
Lane

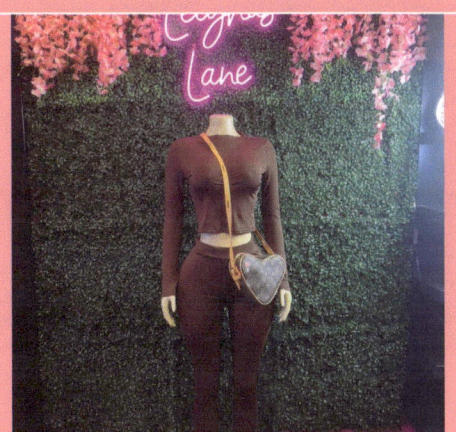

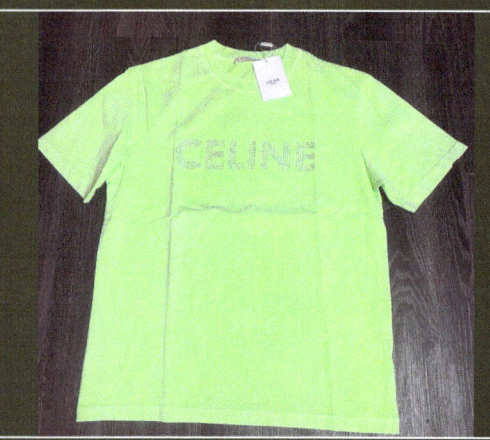

Welcome to United Nutrition, the ideal source for deliciously healthy shakes and energetic drinks. United Nutrition, located in the heart of the community, is more than simply a smoothie and juice bar; it's a lifestyle destination for those who value wellbeing and energy. Whether you're on your way to work or getting ready for a tough workout, United Nutrition provides everything you need to fuel your day with nutritious and delicious options.

Every smoothie and tea at United Nutrition is made with high-quality ingredients to guarantee you get the most nutritional value without sacrificing flavor. Among the standouts is the Salted Caramel Cheesecake Shake, a sumptuous blend that combines enjoyment and wellness with each drink. It's the ideal treat to satiate your sweet craving while helping you stay on track with your fitness objectives. The Tea Bombs are a must-try for individuals in need of an energy boost. These vivid, nutrient-dense teas provide a delightful pick-me-up, loaded with vitamins and antioxidants to keep you going all day.

UNITED NUTRITON

13457 BUSINESS CENTER DRIVE NW ELK RIVER, MN, 55330

(763) 355-9557

The menu at United Nutrition includes more than just shakes and drinks. For the daring palate, they provide a variety of boba cocktails that add a fun and delicious twist to classic beverages. Each boba tea is a symphony of flavors and textures, featuring chewy tapioca pearls and a diverse range of flavor combinations that will keep you going back for more. It's a unique feature that distinguishes United Nutrition from other smoothie bars, providing something for everyone, from health aficionados to those searching for a tasty treat.

United Nutrition is more than simply a location to get a drink; it's a communal hub that prioritizes health and happiness. The cheerful and educated staff is always ready to assist you in selecting the best drink for your needs, whether you're looking for post-workout recovery, a morning boost, or an afternoon treat. United Nutrition is your one-stop shop for everything tasty and healthy, with a focus on quality, health, and great customer service. Visit today to see why it's the best place for shakes, teas, and so much more.

The DETHRONED Cinderella

Poem By Kristy Parque

She was a princess that had a festival of hearts
The shoe used to fit but now it's lighting the spark
Her heart was once warm but now it's like a car that
won't start
Waiting 2 yrs 2 months for him to play his part
Went to the ball but got treated like
The dethroned Cinderella
He Said
2 years 2 months of love on a horizon
Heart breaks, the sun rises
False promises and demises
Beauty surfaces and the lie is
You were my only princess, you're a goddess
I'll dress you in Prada and designer
Buy you a home
Give you my seed that's a reminder
Of our journey to happiness
2 yrs 2 months
Happiness, can you find her ?
Promises, please don't blind her?
Trust me, I'll be kinder
Love me too
Remind her that my hearts a piano
With no keys
You were the sun, but the dog got off the leash Told you
I loved you
She stood with me like no other
Promised you'd be a mother
What's the name of our child

But life got too hard, I want to back down
Abandoned her the moment I touched down
Chose a fan out the crowd
Settled for less where's, my happiness now Becky took
me from her
With a blonde wig and a smile.
I'll betray you like Judas, but the truth is
I shitted on your heart for her
And you got the bruise. 2 yrs 2 months
I'll give you blues
The Dethroned Cinderella
Caught off guard, social media took a hit to her heart
I was selfish, just wanted her to press start
Took everything from her
Annihilated her heart
2 years 2 months of love on the horizon
Heart breaks, the sun rises
False promises and demises
Beauty surfaces and the lie is
You were my only princess, you're a goddess
I'll dress you in Prada and designer
Buy you a home and give you my seed
That's a reminder of our journey to happiness
2 yrs 2 months
Happiness, can you find her ?
Promises, please don't blind her?
Trust me, I'll be kinder
Love me to reminder
But I love me more
She's the dethroned Cinderella
Cause I promised her the world
Told her that she'l

Disticor Magazine Distribution Services and its sister company Disticor Direct distribute over 4,000 magazine titles to newsstand throughout Canada and the United States.

● ● ●

DISTICOR MAGAZINES

Getting magazines onto the right racks and into the right hands is DISTICOR'S strength. With decades of experience in the periodical distribution business, Disticor is now the only Canadian based national distributor of newsstand publications and the second largest national distributor in the USA. Our dedicated team of professionals and state of the art technology will help you navigate the ever-changing newsstand landscape.

DISTICOR

MAGAZINE DISTRIBUTION SERVICES INC

Disticor Magazine Distribution Services Inc., owned by John and Mark Lanfranier, is a leading force in the magazine distribution industry. This privately held firm has established a formidable reputation for excellence and innovation, with a significant presence in both national and international markets. With a strong infrastructure and a great awareness of the shifting environment of print media, Disticor has become a trusted partner for publishers looking for efficient and dependable distribution services.

Disticor has made significant progress under the innovative leadership of the Lanfranier brothers. The Financial Post named the organization one of the "Top 50 Best Managed Private Companies" for its commitment to operational excellence and strategic expansion. This award recognizes Disticor's commitment to sustaining excellent management and service delivery standards, distinguishing it in a competitive industry.

Their creative method to distribution has also been recognized by prestigious organizations. EY nominated the organization for the Canadian Information Productivity Award, recognizing its achievements in harnessing technology to improve productivity and service quality. Disticor's reputation for innovation was further cemented when company received the Information Innovator of the Year award in Market Expansion, recognizing its effective efforts to increase market reach and improve distribution processes.

Furthermore, Disticor's impact on global trade has received attention. The company received the Global Traders Award for Market Expansion, recognizing its ability to navigate and thrive in foreign markets. This recognition reflects Disticor's strategic vision and effectiveness in creating worldwide collaborations. Disticor Magazine Distribution Services Inc.'s successes demonstrate its continued leadership and innovation in the magazine distribution sector, thanks to John and Mark Lanfranier's persistent commitment to excellence and growth.

ADVERTISEMENT HERE

ADVERTISE WITH SLNP UNSIGNED

33

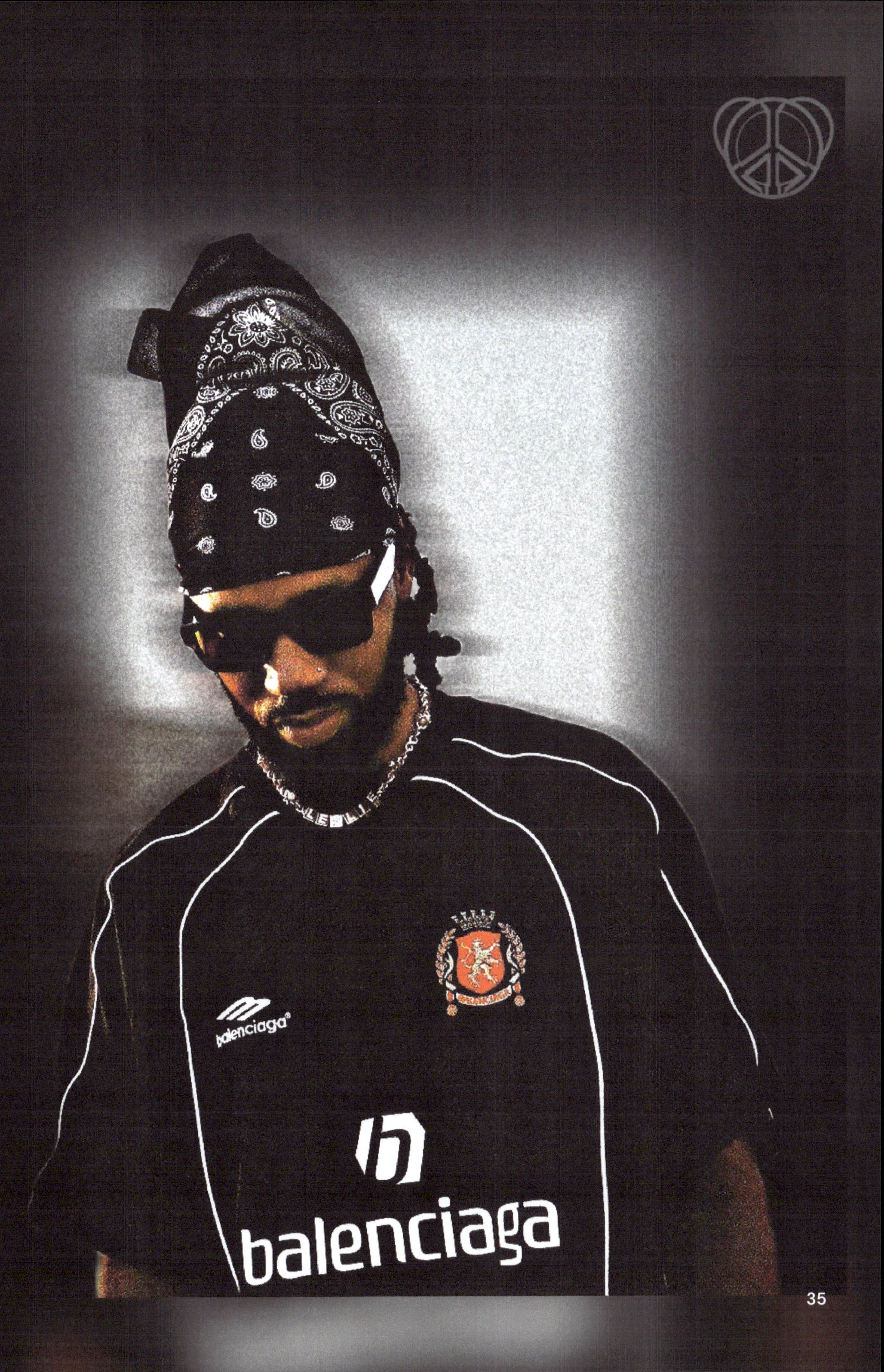
balenciaga
balenciaga

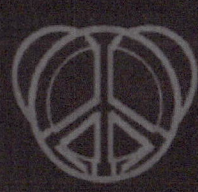

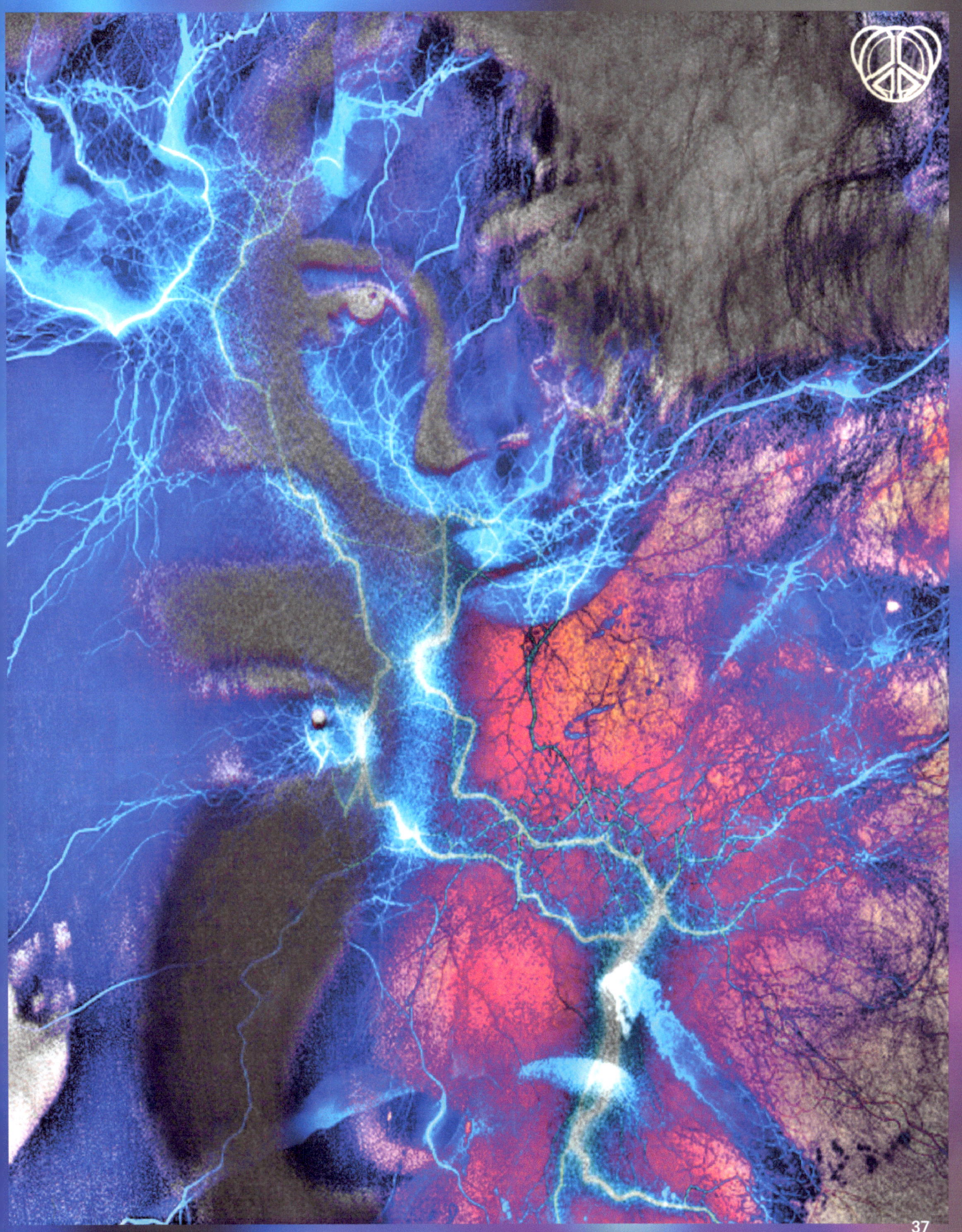

This paperback showcases the undiscovered talents in our very own city! It features artists, musicians, entrepreneurs and innovators who are making their mark in Chicago's creative landscape. Buy a copy of "SLNP Unsigned Vol. 1 Magazine" on Amazon and you too can discover the hidden gems in the Windy City 🏙️ I'm so thankful for the Delightful Infusionz to be featured in this book 🙏✨

https://www.amazon.com/dp/B0CJN3M123/ref=mp_s_a_1_1?crid=DVF0XP2HTBCW&keywords=slnp+unsigned&qid=1695497888&sprefix=slnp+unsigne%252Caps%252C105&sr=8-1

slnp.unsigned

thedelightfulinfusionz

Leighas Lane
Nov 22, 2023 · 🌐

I WAS FEATTURED IN A MAGAZINE FOR MY BOUTIQUE !!!!!

Sn : This guy came in one day and told me he was publishing his own magazine SLNP Art "SLNP UNSIGNED "
asked if I wanted to be apart of it ! I said yes 👏🏾 I LOVE OUR PPL THEY A BRIGHTEN UP YOUR DAY WHEN YOU LEAST EXPECT IT THIS MEAN SO MUCH TO ME CAUSE RUNNING A BUSINESS ISNT EASY 💗

THANK YOU

ashandt_inthecity

slnp.art

slnp.art @slnp.unsigned Vol. 3 Out Now In Bio ❗❗❗🔥🔥 🔥😭😭😭...

@slnp.art wrote a piece on yours truly in their newest volume! be sure to follow them for features of other Chicago locals!

🔗 READ HERE!

 **Poetry Soulchild** is 🤓 feeling blessed with ⸀ ⸰⸰ and **95 others** in **Chicago, IL.** ·

Follow

Feb 10 · 🌐

Shout out to my cousin Bryan Holland for putting me in his SLNP Unsigned Chicago Talent Magazine Volume 3. So please click on the link below to purchase your copy.

https://www.amazon.com/dp/B0CVBKXKWR/ref=mp_s_a_1_4?crid=W2OD05EGR02B&keywords=slnp+art&qid=1707489506&sprefix=slap+art%2Caps%2C156&sr=8-4

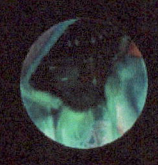

slnp.art
Chicago, Illinois

•••

Post

Liked by **theorchestrationradiostation** and **21 others**

varaydein I'm featured in this month's magazine editon of @slnp.art Unsigned Vol. 4. Make sure you guys head to Amazon.com to check it out

@yadisblossoms

 **yadisblossoms**

@_.YADIII._

Thank You @slnp.art

 **yungmiami305** ✔ 3m ··· ✕

 slnp.art

@yungmiami305 #yungmiami

44

 **Branded Content**

New

 **metroboomin** liked your photo. 32m

 arted following

Follow

 ed your photo. 2h

 ed your photo. 2h

 iked your photo. 2h

 ntioned you in a

.art DaSoul 3h

 Reply

@qveenjourney #SLNP 🏹 💙

qveenjourney

Shop the brand 🛍️ real soft
and warm @slnp.art

Shop with my Cuzzo at SLNP Gallery